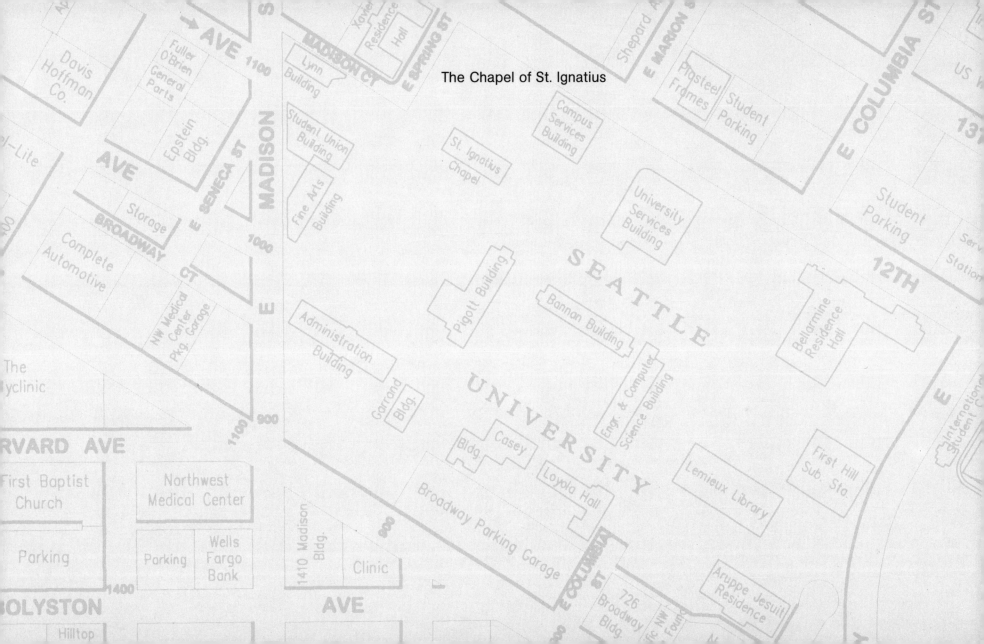

The Chapel of St. Ignatius

The Chapel of St. Ignatius

Steven Holl

WITH AN INTRODUCTION BY
Gerald T. Cobb, S.J.

Princeton Architectural Press, New York

Published by
Princeton Architectural Press
37 East 7th Street
New York, New York 10003
212.995.9620

For a free catalog of books, call 1.800.722.6657
Visit our web site at www.papress.com

Design: Steven Holl and Molly Blieden
Editing and Layout: Clare Jacobson
Cover Design: Sara E. Stemen

Special thanks to: Eugenia Bell, Bernd-Christian Döll, Jane Garvie,
Caroline Green, Therese Kelly, Leslie Ann Kent, Mark Lamster, and Anne
Nitschke of Princeton Architectural Press—Kevin C. Lippert, publisher

Library of Congress Cataloging-in-Publication Data
Holl, Steven.
    The Chapel of St. Ignatius / Steven Holl ; with an introduction by
Gerald T. Cobb.
        p.   cm.
    Includes bibliographical references.
    ISBN 1-56898-180-5 (alk. paper)
    1. St. Ignatius Chapel (Seattle, Wash.) 2. Seattle (Wash.)—Buildings,
structures, etc. I. Title. II. Title: Chapel of Saint Ignatius.
    NA5235.S438H65 1999
    726.5'09797'772—dc21   98-54668
                                                                       CIP

Steven Holl, Architect
Timothy Bade, Project Architect
Rick Sundberg, Tom Kundig, and Jim Graham of
Olson/Sundberg, Local Architects
Baugh Construction
David Gulassa, Metalwork
Doug Hansen, Glasswork
Herve Descottes, Lighting
Salmon Bay, Solid Visions, Woodwork
Linda Beaumont, Art of Chapel of Blessed Sacrament

For Seattle University:
Stephen Sundborg, S.J., President
William J. Sullivan, S.J., Chancellor
Chapel Committee: Gerald T. Cobb, S.J. (Chair), Len Beil, Clara de la
Torre, Terri Gaffney, Rhoady Lee III, Paul Mullally, Mary Romer Cline,
Rev. Michael Ryan, John Whitney, S.J., Martha Wyckoff-Byrne

Visit the Chapel of St. Ignatius web site at www.seattleu.edu/chapel

Contents

Introduction: Sacred Space in the Secular City

Gerald T. Cobb, S.J.

A Vision Renewed

In designing a sacred space for a secular city, Steven Holl drew upon the spiritual and intellectual heritage of St. Ignatius Loyola, the sixteenth-century saint who founded the Society of Jesus, the Jesuits. Ignatius loved the great cities of his time, and whereas mendicant and monastic orders sought locations at the urban gates or far from the city, Ignatius chose more central sites where Jesuits would have access to the poor and also to persons of influence who could support their works of charity and education. Of the approximately seven thousand letters Ignatius wrote in his lifetime, many dealt with the purchase of urban properties for the construction of Jesuit churches, schools, and housing. While he insisted upon utter simplicity for Jesuit residences, Ignatius spared no expense or effort to build landmark churches that would attract large numbers of people for individual reflection and communal worship.

In this spirit Ignatius and the Jesuits initially contracted with Michelangelo in 1553 to build the Church of the Gesu in the heart of Rome. After delays in the project necessitated retaining other architects, the church opened to popular acclaim in 1584. The church's dramatic facade invites people into a space that expresses both a horizontal invitation to a journey toward God and a vertical invitation to be lifted up in an experience of transcendence. The elimination of side aisles brings the worshiping assembly much closer to the liturgy, resulting in what Thomas Lucas calls "the characteristic notes of Jesuit liturgical architecture: a large, single nave that served as an aula for preaching and a shallow sanctuary that stressed the visibility of sacramental activity."[1] Jesuit churches from the first gave great attention not just to the visual impact but also to the acoustical quality of church design because preaching, teaching, and sacred music were principal ways for Jesuits to reach people.[2]

As Jesuit missions spread around the world, the morphology of the Church of the Gesu appeared in far-flung locations such as the Church of La Compania in Cuzco, Peru. Some designs attempted to adapt the architectural style to local cultures, as in the case of the Church of the Holy Savior on the grounds of the Chinese Imperial Palace, where a Chinese gateway and courtyard were added.[3] In 1640 the Jesuit church in Portuguese Macao incorporated into its facade various images of flowers and dragons intended to direct Jesuits' minds and hearts to the rich culture that they would soon enter as missionaries.

Ignatius placed immense importance in architecture because the major turning points in his life were strongly associated with particular locales. His complex spiritual journey from soldier to saint took him from the world of castle and court to the sacred spaces of cave, chapel, and church. His landmark text *The Spiritual Exercises* begins with a "composition of place," in which a person is urged "to see in imagination the physical place where that which I want to contemplate is taking place."[4] In a sense Ignatius became an architect of the spiritual life, engaging all the senses to construct a solid foundation for more idealized values and objectives. Many specific places—the flowing waters of the Cardoner River, the cloistered confines of the caves at Manresa, and the inspirational sacred art of the abbey at Montserrat, Spain—shaped his spiritual perceptions and the ambitious plans that grew out of them.

The Seattle University Context and Process

Ignatius came to the firm conviction that schools and colleges could be powerful instruments for the renewal of cities, so he assigned much of his available manpower to educational ministries. By the time Ignatius died in 1556, the Society of Jesus had 46 colleges; by 1773, there were 669 Jesuit colleges and 196 seminaries throughout the world.[5] Seattle University is one such institution in the Ignatian tradition. Founded in 1891 and located in downtown Seattle, the school is home to approximately 3500 undergraduates and 2500 graduate students in law, education, engineering, nursing, computer science, and theological studies. Students come from a wide array of religious and cultural backgrounds to study in this vibrant Northwest city.

In 1991 the university's president, Fr. William Sullivan, announced his intention to build a chapel that not only would meet the university's needs but also would be an architectural gift to the surrounding civic community. Fr. Sullivan wanted a landmark structure that would take its place among other Seattle landmarks such as the Space Needle. In a letter to the university committee charged with overseeing the chapel project, he wrote, "Let us do something that is aesthetically and liturgically arresting. If we are going to enhance students' religious lives, we must go beyond conventional religious symbols."[6]

A campus committee selected four finalists from among forty firms that submitted portfolios and invited each architect to present a campus lecture on the topic of "Architecture and Sacred Space." After being selected as architect for the chapel project, Steven Holl met extensively with the campus community and also traveled to Montserrat and Rome to do research on the life and thought of St. Ignatius. He engaged in numerous conversations with students about their experience of liturgy and worship, and he unveiled a schematic design and scale model of the proposed chapel on April 4, 1995. The chapel opened two years later, on April 7, 1997.

The chapel's design concept reflects influences and concepts from *The Spiritual Exercises*, which Ignatius wrote as a guidebook for a spiritual director who advises a person through an extended process of personal prayer and discernment. This process assists

St. Ignatius writes the constitutions of his new religious order, the Jesuits. One of five paintings by artist Dora Nikolova Bittau in the chapel narthex.

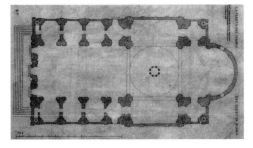

top: Facade of the Church of the Gesu
bottom: Antonio Lafréry, plan of the Church of the Gesu, ca. 1600

the retreatant in discerning among various interior lights and darknesses (Ignatius termed them "consolations" and "desolations") to achieve the inner freedom that will allow him or her to make authentic and just decisions. The Ignatian emphasis upon choosing among constantly shifting interior movements was the primary inspiration for Holl's design concept, "a gathering of different lights." This image eloquently describes both the client and the program for the chapel: the Seattle University community consists of diverse students from around the world, and the program of liturgical worship necessarily involves a processional experience of moving through different moments and places of prayer. The image also underscores two key assumptions of Jesuit education: the community of students and professors will examine issues in different lights, and individuals will employ the light of reason and faith to discern complex questions in their personal and professional lives.

This image of a gathering of different lights was developed further in Holl's concept of seven bottles of light emerging from a stone box. Light passes into the chapel through openings that demarcate interior spaces corresponding to particular moments or aspects of worship. In a powerful paradox Holl has filled these vessels with light that acts like liquid, an aqueous medium spilling across interior surfaces. The play of light and the positioning of windows also transform the chapel's solid forms. For example, the Alaskan cedar

doors at the threshold of the chapel contain seven large glass discs set at different angles into the doors. The discs convey the impression that in some sense the doors are always open forms, pierced or permeated and granting us the power to see through conventional barriers. By day the doors glow with sunlight refracting off hundreds of facets carved into the wood, while at night the doors send light streaming outward through the glass discs in all directions.

In details such as these doors and the rooftop forms that capture and direct light, Holl has richly displayed what the Jesuit anthropologist Teilhard de Chardin calls the "within" of materiality.[7] The haptic or sensory dimension of a building becomes the place of disclosure or revelation of something more than the obvious form: the chiseled surfaces in the Alaskan cedar doors reveal the ligneous interior, which catches and disperses sunlight; light spills and moves across the hand-textured plaster walls; the polished black concrete flooring becomes a reflective watery surface flowing in visual continuity from the pool into the chapel proper. This aliveness at the heart of materiality was described at the liturgy consecrating the chapel when Seattle Archbishop Thomas Murphy quoted the Jesuit poet Gerard Manley Hopkins:

There lives the dearest freshness deep down things;
And though the last lights off the black West went
Oh, morning, at the brown brink eastward, springs—

Because the Holy Ghost over the bent

World broods with warm breast and with ah! bright wings.[8]

The darkness of night gives way, for Hopkins and for Holl, to a renewing sense of illumination, warmth, and soaring heights.

Vessels of Light

The chapel's seven vessels of light invite the worshiper into an ever deeper engagement with the sacred. The first vessel is the processional corridor, which features a lofting high arch filled with white light like a billowing sail; the floor of the corridor slopes gently upward so that the entrant experiences a subtle shift to a higher ground. Just to the right of the processional corridor is the second vessel of light, the narthex. This area for people to gather before or after services also features five paintings from the life of Ignatius and a carpet designed by Holl to depict the spiritual journey of Ignatius. The carpet and paintings summon the observer to use imagination and senses to retrace the journey of Ignatius from Manresa to Cardoner to Paris to Rome.

The other four vessels of light are the nave or main sanctuary where a congregation gathers for worship, the reconciliation chapel where penitent and confessor celebrate the sacrament of God's forgiveness, the choir area from which sacred music emanates, and the chapel of the Blessed Sacrament, a small room for the tabernacle where the Eucharistic bread from mass is reserved for distribution to the sick. Sacred space and sacred time are fused in Holl's design, because each vessel of light illumines a place that has a particular moment in a ritual continuity. As Fr. Sullivan remarked, "The Jesuits have never believed that one's relationship to God happens in one moment."[9]

Steven Holl considers the chapel's seventh vessel of light to be the bell tower that beckons all people into a sense of pilgrimage or sacred procession. The tower is surrounded by a grass "thinking field" and a reflection pool, two important extensions of the chapel's sites for prayer and reflection. Taken together, the tower, field, and pool break the campus's preexisting street grid system by obtruding halfway onto the pedestrian mall so as to interrupt and invite passersby rather dramatically into a moment of contemplation as they walk past. The care given to these elements helps to negate or transcend the artificial boundaries between interior and exterior, sacred and secular, the within and the without. One may argue that the chapel also transcends even the distinction between self and other, person and building, because at the threshold of the chapel of the Blessed Sacrament one sees these words engraved in the floor: "We are all the temple of the living God."

Holl's use of light to join discrete liturgical moments to distinct places within and outside the chapel is

Window in the chapel of the Blessed Sacrament. The Jesuit insignia features the first three Greek letters of the name of Jesus.

10

Anointing by oil on a wall of the chapel by Archbishop Murphy on April 7, 1997

especially striking in the context of the history of Christian religious architecture. Early Christian worship began quite simply in homes where scripture and a Eucharistic meal could be shared by a community of believers. By the fourth century this domestic environment evolved into the larger, more public spaces of the basilicas, which "became more a house for God than a house for God's people."[10] Over time the role of the assembly of believers diminished due to the elaborate ornamentation and visual emphasis given to the tabernacle. The bread broken and shared at the table of the Eucharist took a secondary place to the reserved Eucharistic bread in the elevated, highly ornamented tabernacle that typically dominated the nave.

In 1963 the Second Vatican Council sought to restore the earlier emphasis on the liturgical participation of the assembled worshipers: "The general plan of the sacred edifice should be such that in some way it conveys the image of the gathered assembly."[11] The tabernacle was moved to a place of lesser prominence so that during mass the table of the Eucharist and the assembly itself would be the principal visual and symbolic focus. The liturgical life of the community was also to reflect the greater openness of the church toward all people in a spirit of dialogue with believers and nonbelievers. Just as the Church of the Gesu draws believers into a more intimate encounter with preaching and other liturgical experiences, the Chapel of St.

Ignatius emphasizes the congregation's greater participation in the Church after Vatican II. The careful attention given to the exterior precincts of pool and thinking field as integral parts of the chapel site open the chapel to people of all faiths or no faith.

Pedagogical Function

This openness fulfills the mission of Jesuit universities today to create "a place of serene and open search for and discussion of the truth ... the indispensable horizon and context for a genuine preservation, renewal, and communication of knowledge and human values."[12] With its curved and banked wall surfaces, the Chapel of St. Ignatius offers such horizons in a serene and visionary environment. It affords the traditional sanctuary of religious architecture, a place of peace in the hurly-burly of life, but it is an interrogative as well as a declarative space, in the sense that it provokes a kind of pedagogical wonder, as one student reveals in a description of her first visit to the chapel: "I was like a child—both awestruck and excited to ask my questions. I could not figure out where all the light was coming from and how did all those colors come through clear windows? How was there so much life there?"[13]

The pedagogical engagement of the observer begins with an initial dissonance between the exterior structure of the chapel, with its massive tablets of ochre-stained concrete, and the interior, which features carefully textured plaster walls that curve, vault, and soar in haunting beauty. The exterior strikes some viewers as spare and ascetic, conveying a contemporary sense of *gravitas* that is shorn of trivial ornament and that suggests both a solidarity with surrounding urban buildings and also a sense of radical difference. The interior, by contrast, imparts a contemporary sense of curvilinear richness and the extravagant generosity of simple materials. Fr. Sullivan commented during the chapel's inaugural mass, "Just as you cannot dictate the shape of a person's relation to the Transcendent, so you cannot judge that relation—its richness, its depth, its intensity—by the outward appearance. The lives of the saints are filled with examples of men and women who were uncultured, unconventional, unwashed. And yet at the heart of those lives shone the light of grace, lights of brilliant color and intensity."[14]

Pedagogical growth requires change, and consequently the chapel is filled with sites of shifting identity, demonstrating that a destabilized symbol is, in general, a more engaging symbol. For example, Holl designed solid bronze legs to anchor the altar table, the central focus for liturgical worship. As an observer moves within the chapel, the apparent fixity of the altar legs dissolves into a deeper mystery as the bronze supports take on new shapes because of the observer's changing vantage point. When one finally reaches the center aisle one sees that the legs have assumed the shapes of alpha and omega, the first and last letters of the Greek alphabet. This is a significant moment inspired by the

Book of Revelation, in which Jesus asserts, "I am the Alpha and the Omega, the first and the last, the beginning and the end."[15] Holl's epiphanic design in this instance offers a tangible vision of the promise of Jesus to be present in the celebration of the worshiping community gathered around the altar.

The altar provides one example of a recurring phenomenon, since perceptions of the chapel alter whenever observers shift their position within the space. As sunlight spills into the chapel, the grooved wall surface in some places comes alive in sharp relief while in other places it recedes into a smooth and soothingly plain surface. The chapel marks time in a different way, just as the liturgical calendar of the church year and the rhythm of the liturgical rites draw people into a sense of sacred time.

Roland Barthes, writing in *Sade, Fourier, Loyola*, sees Ignatius as someone who believed in the power of one object or place to be simultaneously many things.[16] For Barthes, *The Spiritual Exercises* is a profoundly organic and imaginative work, because in effect it is simultaneously four different texts: a text for a retreat director to use, a text adapted for an individual retreatant, an enacted text insofar as the retreatant responds to and carries out the described exercises, and finally an implied fourth text of God's response to the retreatant's prayers. Barthes sees Ignatius's text as a system of thought that elaborates itself in a complex

left: Monastery and hills of Montserrat
above: Black Madonna of Montserrat, 12th century

treelike structure, giving an internal consistency and strength to the methodology that branches off into so many aspects of the spiritual life.

For Barthes, Ignatius was always seeking "an interlocution, i.e., a new language that can circulate between the Divinity and the exercitant."[17] The success of the Chapel of St. Ignatius comes in its achievement of an innovative architectural interlocution between the individual or community and the transcendent. Steven Holl has realized the architectural vision of Ignatius in the concrete setting of Seattle. Robert A. Ivy described the experience of one architect who visited the chapel: "She found herself forced to sit down on first entering the interior, as she was so completely overcome by emotion and memory. The new building acted like a key for her, unlocking a wealth of internal, unspoken language with unanticipated force."[18] This is an example of the engagement Ignatius sought in Jesuit architecture, which he hoped would be innovative and highly responsive to the differences in individuals, while still serving as a compelling landmark or drawing point for the renewal of urban communities in the direction of greater faith and justice.

1. Thomas M. Lucas, S.J., *Landmarking: City, Church and Jesuit Urban Strategy* (Chicago: Loyola Press, 1997), 98.
2. John W. O'Malley, S.J., *The First Jesuits* (Cambridge, MA: Harvard University Press, 1993), 357.
3. Lucas, *Landmarking*, 15.
4. Ignatius Loyola, *The Spiritual Exercises*, trans. George E. Ganss, S.J. (St. Louis: Institute of Jesuit Sources, 1992), 47.
5. Douglas Letson and Michael Higgins, *The Jesuit Mystique* (Chicago: Loyola Press, 1995), 136.
6. William J. Sullivan, S.J., memo to Seattle University Chapel Committee, 1991.
7. Pierre Teilhard de Chardin, S.J., *The Heart of Matter* (New York: Harcourt Brace Jovanovich, 1976), 15.
8. Gerard Manley Hopkins, S.J. "God's Grandeur," *The Poems of Gerard Manley Hopkins*, 4th ed., ed. W. H. Gardner and N. H. MacKenzie (Oxford: Oxford University Press, 1970), 66.
9. Quoted in Marsha King, "Little Church at Seattle U. is a Big Deal Architecturally," *The Seattle Times*, 11 December, 1996, p. A17.
10. Thomas G. Simons and James M. Fitzpatrick, *The Ministry of Liturgical Environment* (Collegeville, MN, Liturgical Press, 1978), 13.
11. U.S. Catholic Conference of Bishops, *The General Instruction of the Roman Missal* (New York: Catholic Book Publishing Company, 1974) 41.
12. John L. McCarthy, S.J., ed., *Documents of the Thirty-Fourth General Congregation of the Society of Jesus* (Saint Louis: Institute of Jesuit Sources, 1995), 191.
13. Quoted in "Personal Reflections on the Chapel of St. Ignatius," *Broadway and Madison Newsletter*, 5 May 1997, p. 3.
14. William J. Sullivan, S.J., "Sermon for the Inaugural Mass," pamphlet (23 March 1997).
15. Rev. 22:13.
16. Roland Barthes, *Sade, Fourier, Loyola*, trans. Richard Miller (New York: Hill and Wang, 1976), 41.
17. Ibid., 4.
18. Robert A. Ivy, "Building Sanctuary," *Architectural Record* (April 1998): 15.

A Gathering of Different Lights

Steven Holl

In the winter of 1991 Father William Sullivan planned to build a chapel dedicated to St. Ignatius. Father Sullivan envisioned a new center for spiritual life at Seattle University that would provide a contemporary interpretation of Jesuit tradition.

While interviewing for the commission, I presented our work in a lecture entitled "Questions of Perception," which described a phenomenology of architecture. The lecture argued for a heightened development of spatial and experiential dimensions through individual reflection on the senses and perception. To open ourselves to perception, we must transcend the mundane urgency of "things to do." We must try to access that inner life that reveals the luminous intensity of the world. Only through solitude can we begin to penetrate the secrets around us. An awareness of one's unique existence in space is essential in developing a consciousness of perception.

Architecture holds the power to inspire and transform our day-to-day existence. The everyday act of pressing a door handle and entering into a light-washed room can become profound when experienced through sensitized consciousness. To see, to feel these physicalities is to become a subject of the senses. As Goethe has remarked, "One should not seek anything behind the phenomena, they are lessons themselves."

At the time of my lecture I had not yet realized the connection between this phenomenological approach to architecture and related writings by St. Ignatius that were embraced by the Jesuit school's campus ministry staff. St. Ignatius of Loyola's *The Spiritual Exercises*, printed in 1548, argued for a philosophical interpretation of the senses. This work, preceding later writings on phenomenology by three hundred years, reorders the hierarchy of the five senses. Hearing becomes the most refined sense while sight—the traditionally dominant sense—comes third after touch. The phenomenal teachings of St. Ignatius became a primary source of inspiration as Tim Bade and I studied and worked on the design.

In his introduction, Father Cobb describes how "Ignatius placed immense importance in architecture because the major turning points in his life were strongly associated with particular locales." St. Ignatius of Loyola's life chronicles an interior history of mystical experiences from the Black Madonna of Manresa, where he laid down his sword to Cardoner, to the Ignatian rooms at Il Gesu in Rome. (During the course of the project I was able to visit these sites and experience their importance in the Jesuit tradition.) On the rainy day of my visit to Manresa (one hour north of Barcelona) I remember the power of the foggy mist that blew over the strange rocky cliffs above the monastery. The local myth was like a fairy tale; these cliffs of stone were once smooth. They suddenly became serrated the day Christ was crucified. The Black Madonna at this site is a black-stained wooden sculpture; in her outstretched hand the orb of the earth is worn smooth by repeated touching.

In *The Spiritual Exercises*, St. Ignatius continually refers to a particular metaphor of light, "the light to perceive what can best be decided upon must

"he returns to his metaphore of LIGHT, the
light to perceive what can best be decided
upon must come down from the first AND
Supreme Wisdom." Exercises of St. Ignatius

come down [from above]." St. Ignatius wrote about darkness and light—"consolation" and "desolation"—and insisted that desolation can in fact be an experience of growth. My early sketches for the Chapel of St. Ignatius aim to describe spaces billowing up with light coming in through folds from above—a caesura of waves in the emerald light of the morning sun.

The concept for the chapel began to form as "a gathering of different lights." This double entendre referred to the many different nationalities of students brought together at Seattle University. It also referred to the elements of the Jesuit liturgical program for the chapel, shown in the concept sketch "Seven Bottles of Light in a Stone Box." In this sketch, each bottle of light corresponds to a program element: the narthex, the procession hall, the main gathering space, the reconciliation chapel, the choir, and the chapel of the Blessed Sacrament. The seventh bottle of light is the bell tower with its blast of night light over the reflecting pond.

The campus ministry supported the concept completely. When, at a time of cost reduction pressures, the campus physical planners tried to reduce the number of bottles to four, the campus ministry refused. "There are seven bottles, there are seven days," they said. The concept for the chapel had become clear. The work of realizing it in material and detail would take two more years and hundreds of drawings.

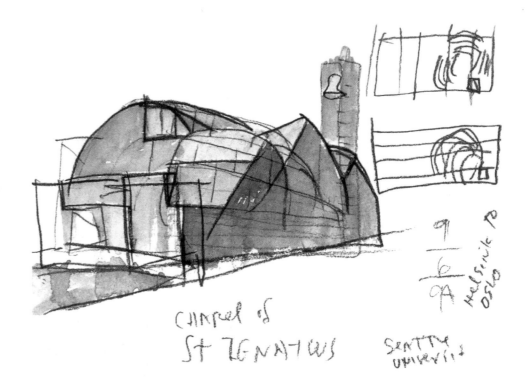

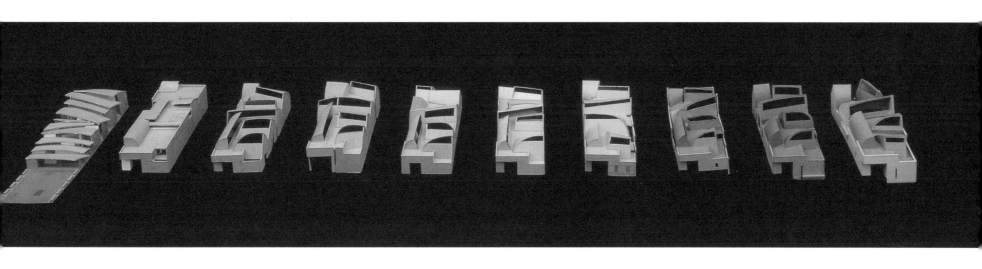

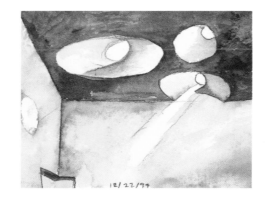

The angst of a concept before spatial definition: interior and exterior are simultaneously explored.

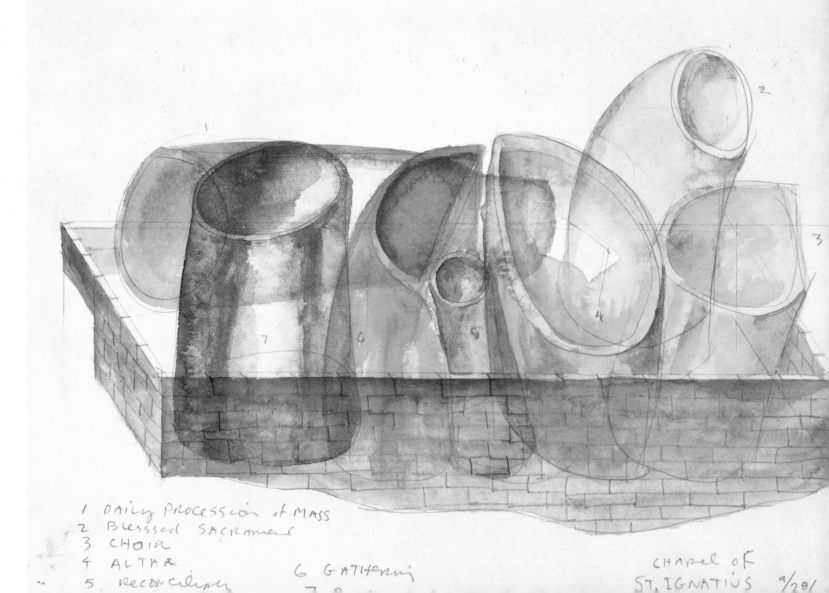

7 Different Bottles of Light
in a stone box

1 Daily Procession of Mass
2 Blessed Sacrament
3 Choir
4 Altar
5 Reconciling
6 Gathering

Chapel of
St. Ignatius 9/28/

18

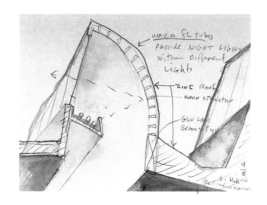

WARM FL TUBES
PROVIDE NIGHT LIGHT
within Different
LIGHTS

ZINC Roof
WOOD STRUCTURE

GLU LAM
BEAM Type

S. Holl
Bernadino Nativus

CANDLE OFFERING AREA
AFTER FUNER

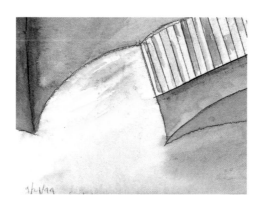

1/4/99

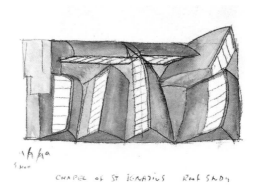

1/4/99
S. Holl

CHAPEL OF ST IGNATIUS   ROOF STUDY

"Bottles"?

10/27/94
S. Holl   CHAPEL OF ST. IGNATIUS

20

"The whole universe is aflame."
—Pierre Teilhard de Chardin
Hymn of the Universe

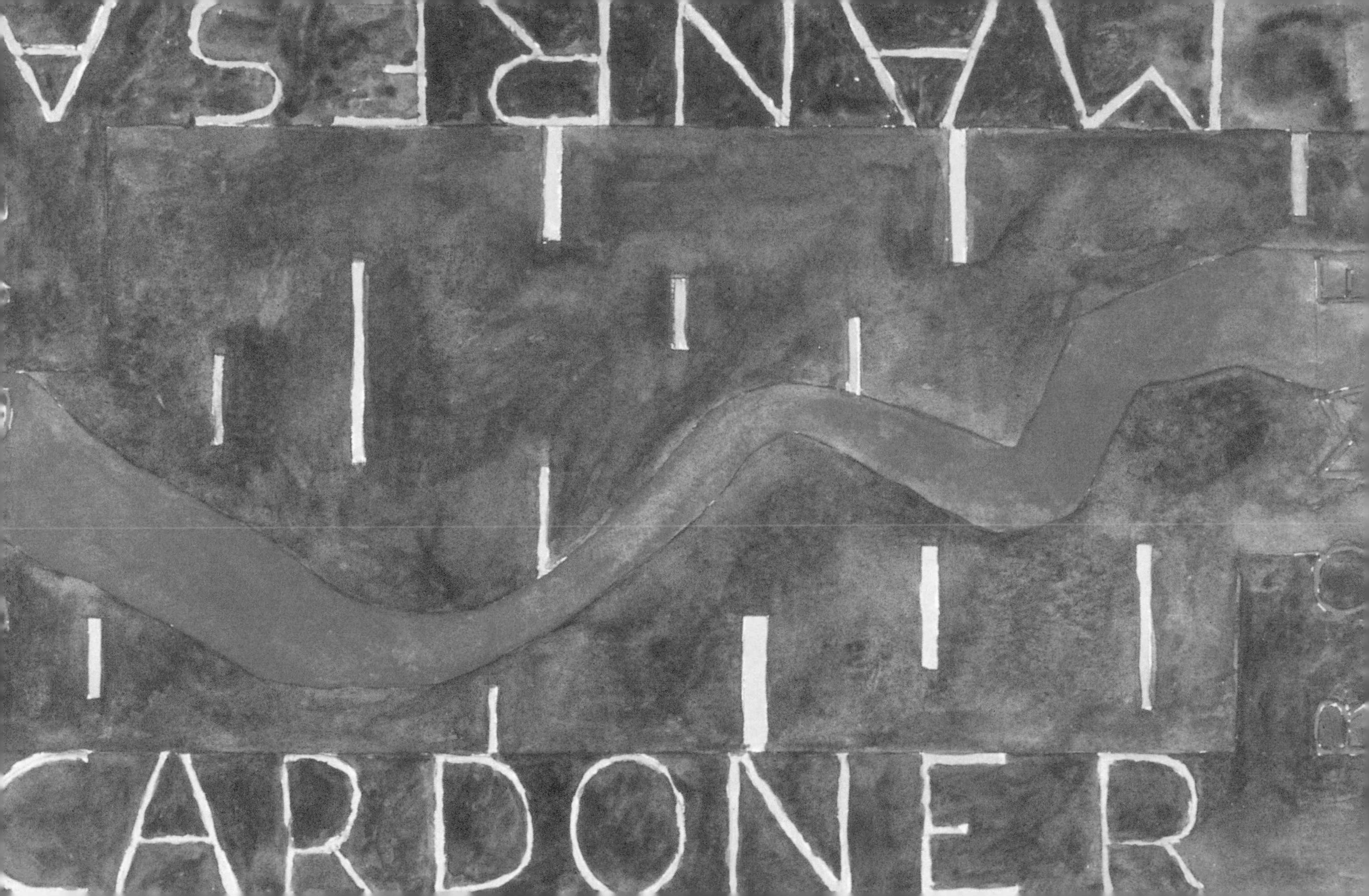
MANRESA
CARDONER

Worm's-eye view of preliminary study

"Within every being and every event there is a progressive expansion of a
mysterious inner clarity which transfigures them."
          —Pierre Teilhard de Chardin, *The Heart of Matter*

Vision

Elements of the city, the university, and the chapel are each embodied in the building scheme. The Seattle University campus was planned on existing urban blocks. We addressed the need for common green space by siting the chapel in the center of a former street and elongating the building plan. New green campus quadrangles were formed to the north, west, and south, and a future quadrangle is planned to the east.

Thematically, the "bottles of light emerging from a stone box" are expressed in the ground plan. Each of the light volumes matches a part of the mass. The city-facing north light corresponds to the chapel of the Blessed Sacrament and to the mission of Seattle University's outreach to the community. A volume of east and west light fills the main space, used for worship. The worship space was to be designed "in the round," as favored by the Second Vatican Council, while the procession called for an elongated space; the plan merges these two distinct forms into one space with a defined procession as well as a surrounded altar.

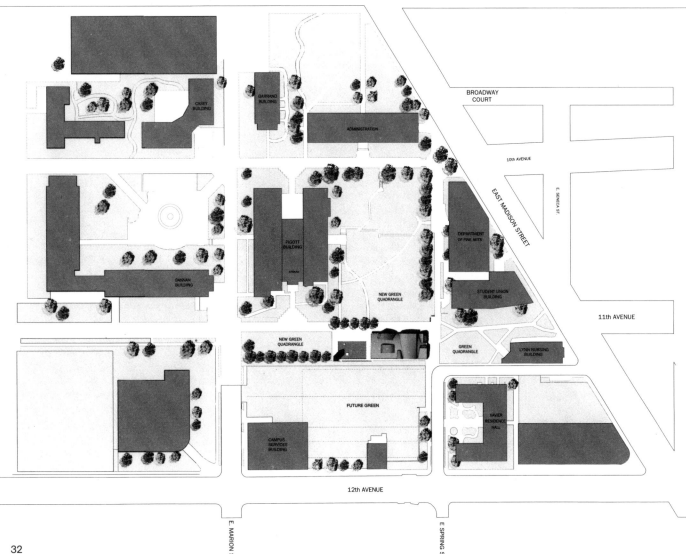

BROADWAY

CASEY
BUILDING

GARRAND
BUILDING

ADMINISTRATION

BROADWAY
COURT

10th AVENUE

E. SENECA ST.

EAST MADISON STREET

BANNAN
BUILDING

PIGOTT
BUILDING

ATRIUM

NEW GREEN
QUADRANGLE

DEPARTMENT
OF FINE ARTS

STUDENT UNION
BUILDING

11th AVENUE

NEW GREEN
QUADRANGLE

GREEN
QUADRANGLE

LYNN NURSING
BUILDING

FUTURE GREEN

XAVIER
RESIDENCE
HALL

CAMPUS
SERVICES
BUILDING

12th AVENUE

E. MARION ST.

E SPRING ST.

32

facing page: Chapel plan
Liturgical furniture legend

1. altar
2. ambo
3. president's chair
4. deacon/minister chair
5. acolyte seating
6. cantor's stand
7. candle stand
8. paschal candle stand
9. ambry for holy oils
10. processional cross
11. candle for book
12. stand for book
13. ancillary tables
14. vessels for mass
15. vessels for holy oils
16. fixed cross
17. pews
18. movable chairs
19. choir chairs
20. tabernacle
21. tabernacle stand
22. tabernacle lamp
23. chairs for meditation
24. prie-dieu
25. candle offering
26. confessor's chair
27. penitent's chair
28. penitent's prie-dieu
29. movable privacy screen
30. table/book stand
31. carpet
32. brochure rack
33. bench
34. clock
35. sacrarium
36. censer cabinet
37. vesting table
38. chairs
39. patron shrine
40. vanity table
41. vanity stools

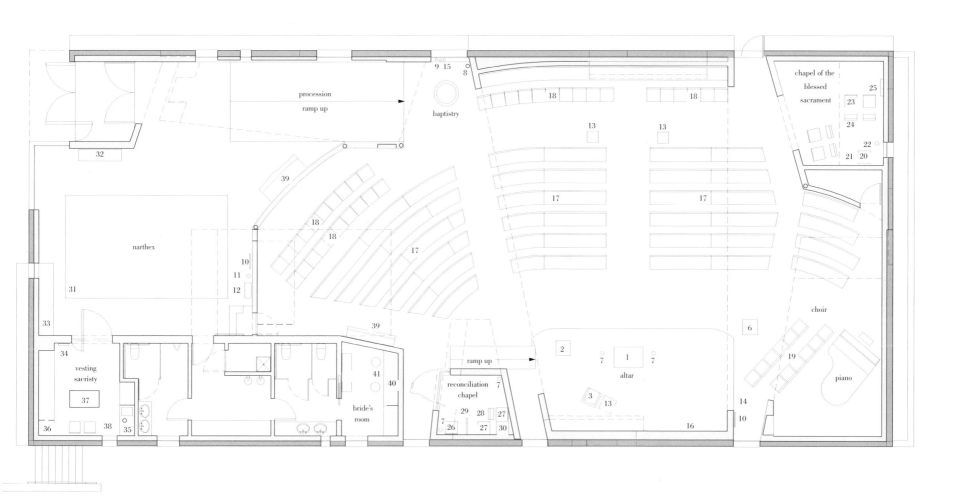

procession ramp up

9 15
8

baptistry

18   18

13   13

17   17

chapel of the
blessed
sacrament

25

23

24

22

21 20

32

39

18

18

10

11

12

narthex

31

17

17

choir

6

33

34

vesting
sacristy

37

39

41

40

ramp up

2

7   1   7

altar

19

piano

36   38

35

bride's
room

reconciliation
chapel

29   28   27

7   26   27   30

7

14

3   13

10

16

33

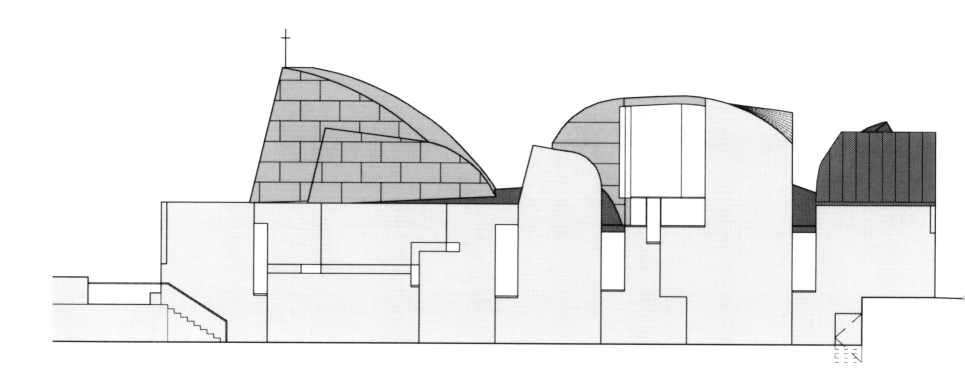

34

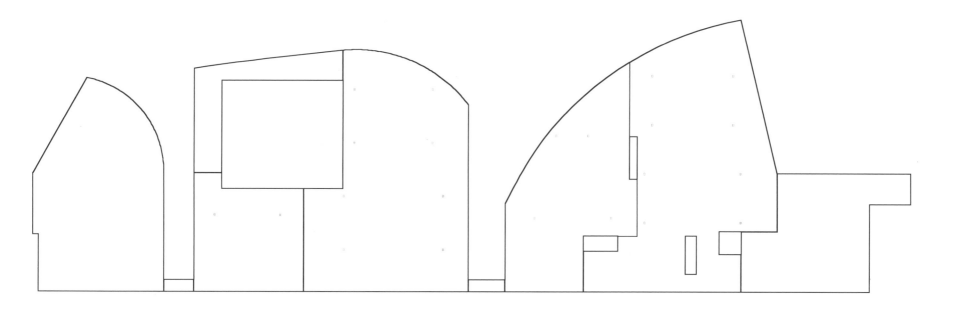

facing page: East elevation study

above: West elevation—the "stone box" made of twenty-one tilt-up concrete slabs with pick pocket points located to distribute the load evenly for the lift

right: Study and final pick pocket point plugs

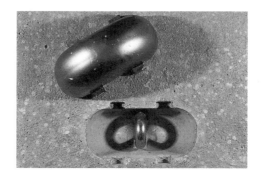

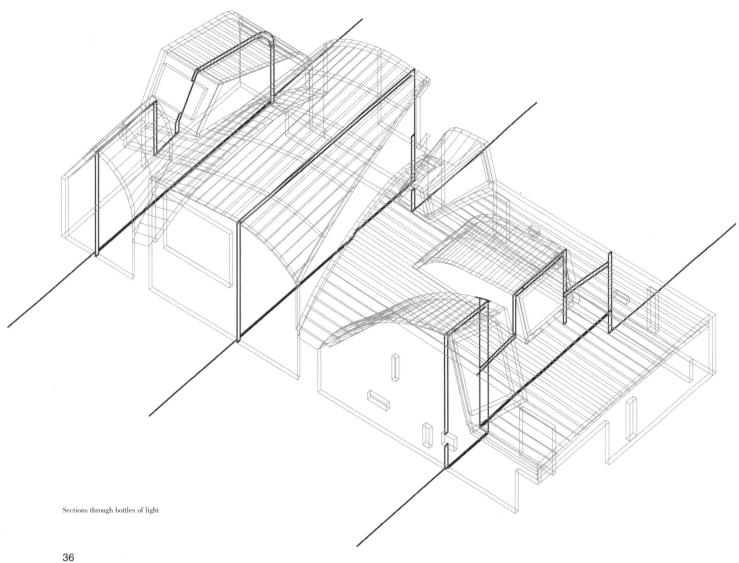

Sections through bottles of light

The acoustics of the space are shaped for both chamber and vocal music by focusing the radial point of the curved roof either below the floor or above the human ear. The acoustics of the space are so effective that an electronic amplifying system is not necessary.

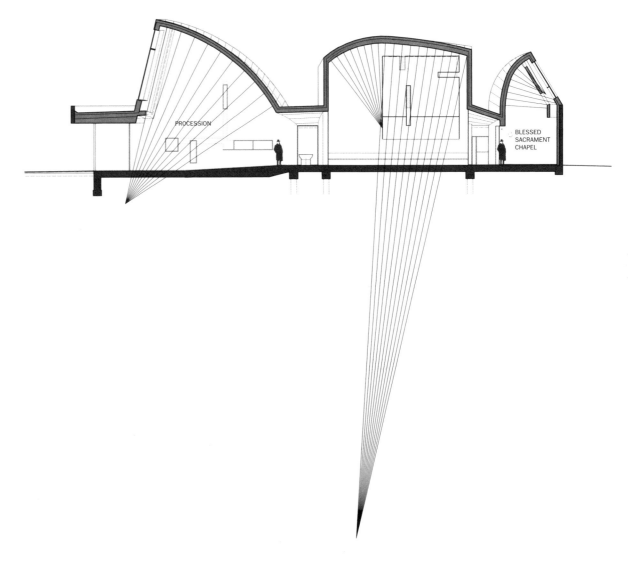

PROCESSION

BLESSED SACRAMENT CHAPEL

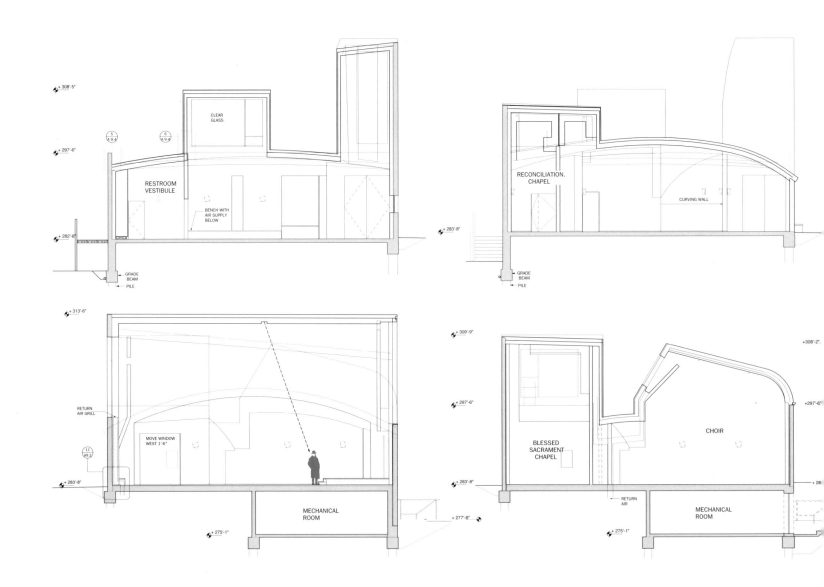

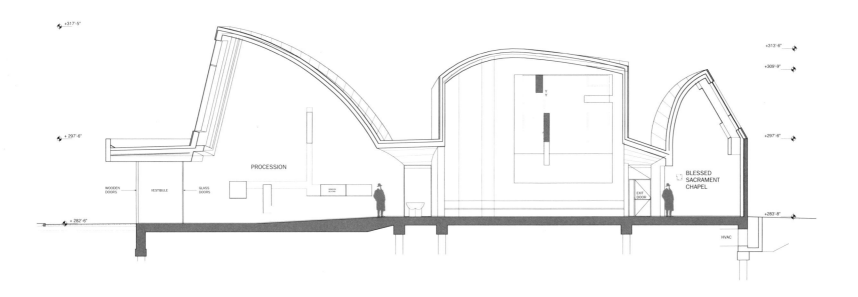

+317'-5"

+313'-6"

+309'-9"

+ 297'-6"

+297'-6"

PROCESSION

BLESSED
SACRAMENT
CHAPEL

WOODEN
DOORS

VESTIBULE

GLASS
DOORS

EXIT
DOOR

+ 282'-6"

+283'-8"

HVAC

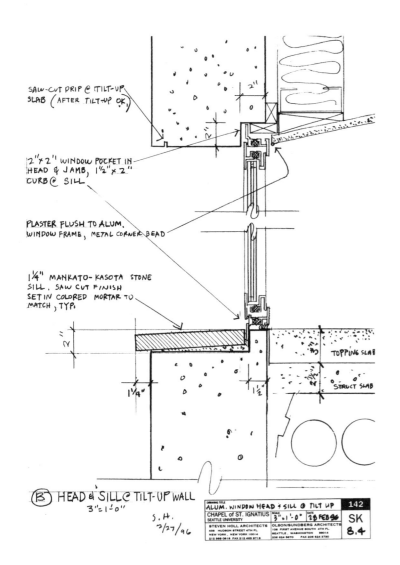

SAW-CUT DRIP @ TILT-UP
SLAB (AFTER TILT-UP OK)

2"x 2" WINDOW POCKET IN
HEAD & JAMB, 1½"x 2"
CURB @ SILL

PLASTER FLUSH TO ALUM.
WINDOW FRAME, METAL CORNER BEAD

1¼" MANKATO-KASOTA STONE
SILL, SAW CUT FINISH
SET IN COLORED MORTAR TO
MATCH, TYP.

2"

1¼"   1½"   2½"

TOPPING SLAB

STRUCT SLAB

Ⓑ HEAD & SILL @ TILT-UP WALL
3"=1'-0"

S.H.
7/27/96

DRAWING TITLE ALUM. WINDOW HEAD & SILL @ TILT UP	142
CHAPEL of ST. IGNATIUS SEATTLE UNIVERSITY	SCALE 3"=1'-0" DATE 28 FEB 96	SK 8.4
STEVEN HOLL ARCHITECTS 435 HUDSON STREET 4TH FL NEW YORK, NEW YORK 10014 212 989 0918 FAX 212 463 9718	OLSON/SUNDBERG ARCHITECTS 108 FIRST AVENUE SOUTH 4TH FL SEATTLE, WASHINGTON 98014 206 624 5670 FAX 206 624 3730	

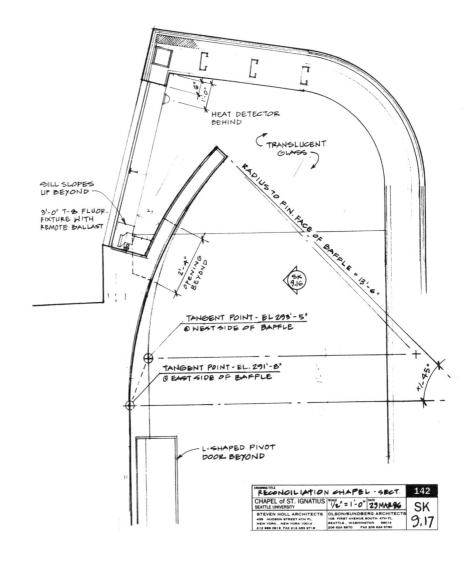

HEAT DETECTOR
BEHIND

TRANSLUCENT
GLASS

RADIUS TO FIN. FACE OF BAFFLE = 13'-6"

SILL SLOPES
UP BEYOND

3'-0" T-8 FLUOR.
FIXTURE WITH
REMOTE BALLAST

2'-4"
OPENING
BEYOND

SK
9.16

TANGENT POINT - EL 293'-5"
@ WEST SIDE OF BAFFLE

TANGENT POINT - EL 291'-8"
@ EAST SIDE OF BAFFLE

45°

L-SHAPED PIVOT
DOOR BEYOND

DRAWING TITLE RECONCILIATION CHAPEL - SECT.	142
CHAPEL of ST. IGNATIUS SEATTLE UNIVERSITY	SCALE ½"=1'-0" DATE 29 MAR 96	SK 9.17
STEVEN HOLL ARCHITECTS 435 HUDSON STREET 4TH FL NEW YORK, NEW YORK 10014 212 989 0918 FAX 212 463 9718	OLSON/SUNDBERG ARCHITECTS 108 FIRST AVENUE SOUTH 4TH FL SEATTLE, WASHINGTON 98014 206 624 5670 FAX 206 624 3730	

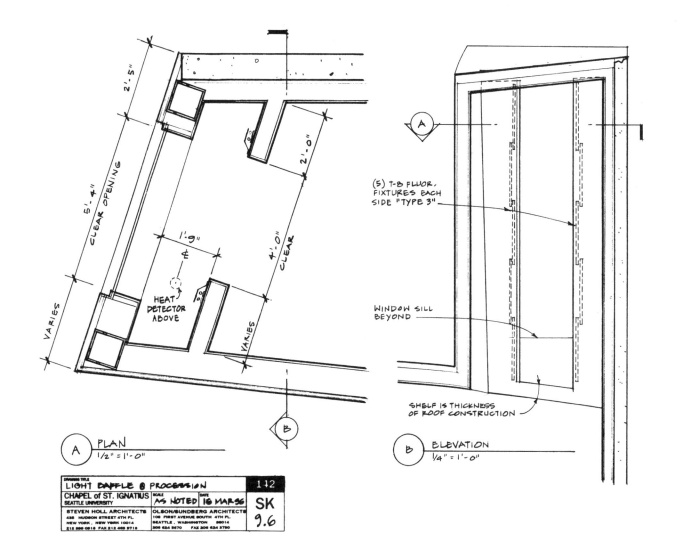

2'-5"

CLEAR OPENING

5'-4"

2'-0"

VARIES

1'-9"

4'-0" CLEAR

HEAT
DETECTOR
ABOVE

VARIES

(5) T-8 FLUOR.
FIXTURES EACH
SIDE "TYPE 3"

WINDOW SILL
BEYOND

SHELF IS THICKNESS
OF ROOF CONSTRUCTION

Ⓐ PLAN
1/2" = 1'-0"

Ⓑ ELEVATION
1/4" = 1'-0"

DRAWING TITLE		1-2
LIGHT BAFFLE @ PROCESSION		
CHAPEL of ST. IGNATIUS	SCALE AS NOTED	DATE 16 MAR 96	SK 9.6
SEATTLE UNIVERSITY		
STEVEN HOLL ARCHITECTS	OLSON/SUNDBERG ARCHITECTS	
435 HUDSON STREET 4TH FL.	108 FIRST AVENUE SOUTH 4TH FL.	
NEW YORK, NEW YORK 10014	SEATTLE, WASHINGTON 98014	
212 989 0918 FAX 212 463 9718	206 624 5670 FAX 206 624 3730	

Realization

The "stone box" of the chapel itself is constructed of twenty-one concrete tilt-up slabs. These slabs were poured horizontally, cured for eighteen days, and then raised in only twelve hours. At the building's four corners, the tilt-up slabs interlock like a Chinese box to expose the load-bearing thickness of the concrete. Window openings are formed when cuts at the slab joints engage as the slabs are tilted into place. Integral-color tilt-up concrete slabs define a tectonic more direct and far more economical than stone veneer. Father Sullivan and I watched the tilt-up operation together with a certain joy. The structural body of the chapel rose up suddenly from the campus ground like an apparition!

While the famous tilt-up slabs of Rudolph M. Schindler's King's Road House were lifted by block and tackle, at the Chapel of St. Ignatius a sophisticated multiple-boom crane lifted, turned, and placed pieces weighing as much as 80,000 pounds. Embedded in the walls, "pick-pocket" points used for lifting and balancing the slabs remain intentionally visible on the building's exterior. These points are capped with special cast bronze protective covers.

The curved roof spaces of the bottles of light are made using pre-bent steel tubes that rest on the tilt-up walls. The merging of the wall and the ceiling of the interiors is shaped in metal lathe and hand-troweled scratch-coat plaster. The polished patina of the concrete floors reflects the light from the bottles, sometimes bouncing it back to the walls.

Bent tubes roof framing

above: The largest tilt-up slab weighs 80,000 pounds and is filled with
reinforcing steel. Its greatest stress is during the lift.
facing page: A tangle of cables sixty feet in the air stops the most difficult
lift for over two hours in suspense.

facing page: Temporary braces await roof framing

above: Interlocked corners

right: "Apparition"; all the walls are up in twelve hours

Radiance/Illumination

A large reflecting pond was formed directly to the south of the chapel. The shallow water of this pond, which is called the "thinking field" joins with a lawn to the south to form the forecourt for the chapel, providing a new campus space. At night the pond reflects a wash of light from the seventh bottle, the bell tower, and emphasizes the geometry of the space. After nightfall, which is the time when masses are offered in the chapel, the light volumes become beacons shining in all directions out across the university campus. On certain occasions, these lights shine throughout the entire night.

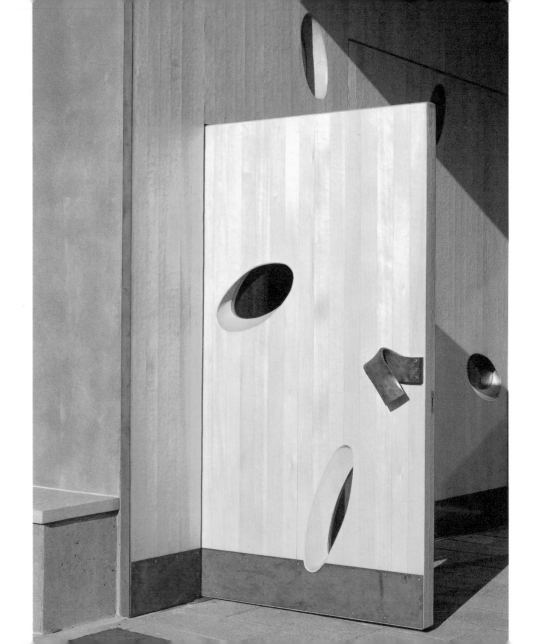

Day of consecration, April 7, 1997

"The apprehension of the absolute in the form of the tangible."
—Teilhand de Chardin, S.J.

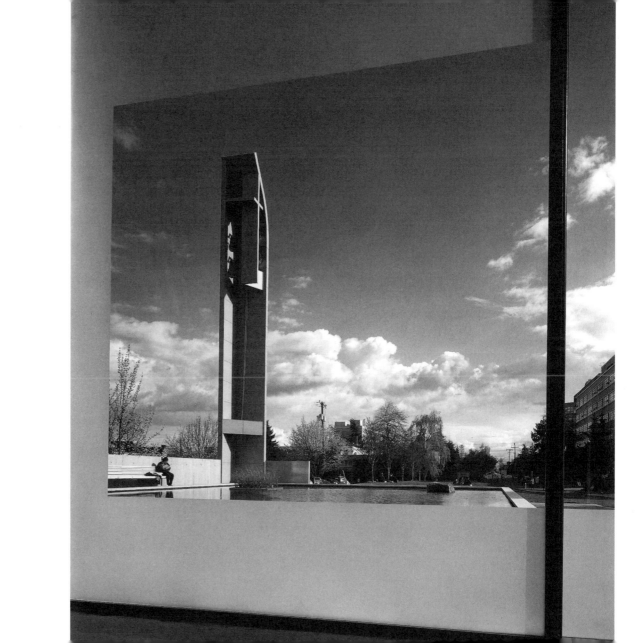

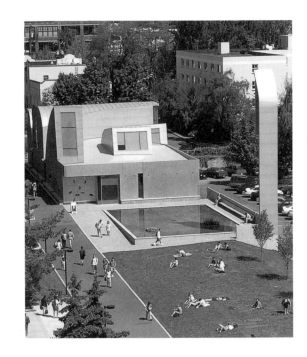

Benches along the west facade face the green quadrangle

The Haptic Realm

St. Ignatius's emphasis on the senses and the haptic realm of touch in *The Spiritual Exercises* are expressed in special handmade and custom-designed furnishings and fixtures for the chapel. Entry doors of Alaskan cedar were carved with lenses to capture seven ovals of sunlight. Bronze door handles, the baptistry, the ambo, the altar, and pews were all designed for the space and built by local craftsmen. Sand-cast glass wall sconces in combination with suspended blown-glass lights complement the light emerging from the baffles. A special smell emanates from the chapel of the Blessed Sacrament, finished in beeswax by the artist Linda Beaumont. Along the procession hall are four fused glass windows crafted by Doug Hanson; each depicts one of the four weeks of the Jesuit spiritual exercises. Water and fire join together in the Easter vigil fire that burns on a block of black granite originating from the glacial summit of nearby Mt. Rainier.

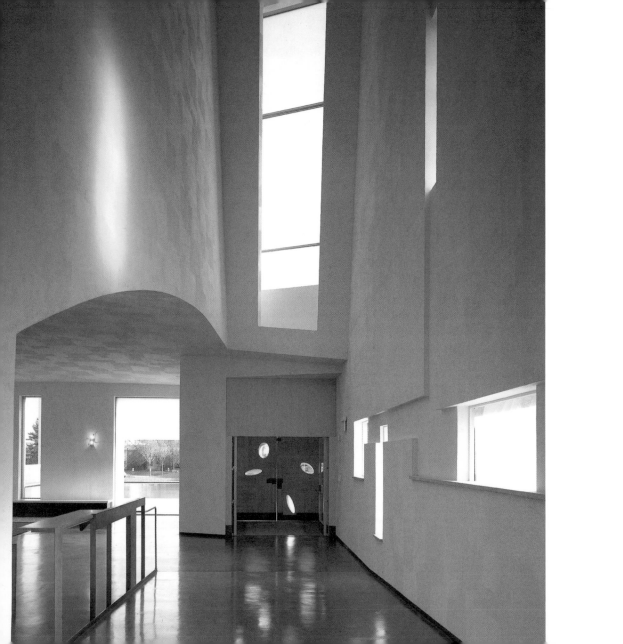

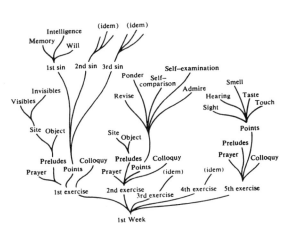

The four windows correspond to the four weeks of *The Spiritual Exercises*.

"We feel unequal to the task, stretched like canvas to a difficult tension, fragile as glass. But bathed in light we find ways to become the light."
　　　—Paul Kidder, "Modern Architecture and Ignatian Vision"

In shadows of shadows darkness is an oblivion awaiting the inspiration of a spot of light

CASSIONNE
CROSS

AMB

10

Carved Alaskan cedar baptismal font with specially cast glass vessels
for holy oils

Altar of the alpha and the omega

Studies in Light

In the narthex and procession hall, the natural light of the sun creates a play of shadows. Moving deeper into the chapel, the light glows mysteriously from the reflected color fields. Each "bottle of light" contains a unique reflected color with a colored lens of a complimentary color. When people stare at a blue rectangle and then a white surface, they will see a yellow rectangle. The twofold merging of concept and phenomena in the chapel is communicated in this visual phenomenon of complementary colors.

The procession is lit by diffused natural sunlight. In the nave a yellow field is combined with a blue lens to the east, and a blue field with a yellow lens to the west. In the chapel of the Blessed Sacrament, an orange field is colored by a purple lens. The choir has a green field with a red lens. The reconciliation chapel combines a purple field with an orange lens. The bell tower and pond both have projected light and reflected natural light.

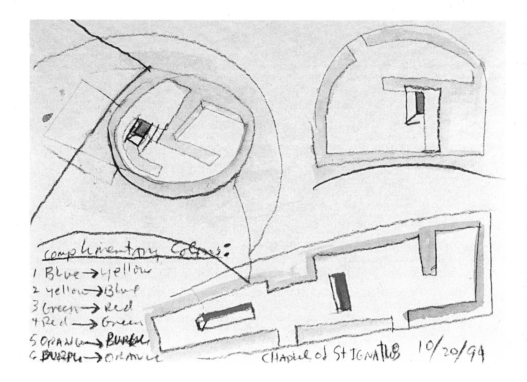

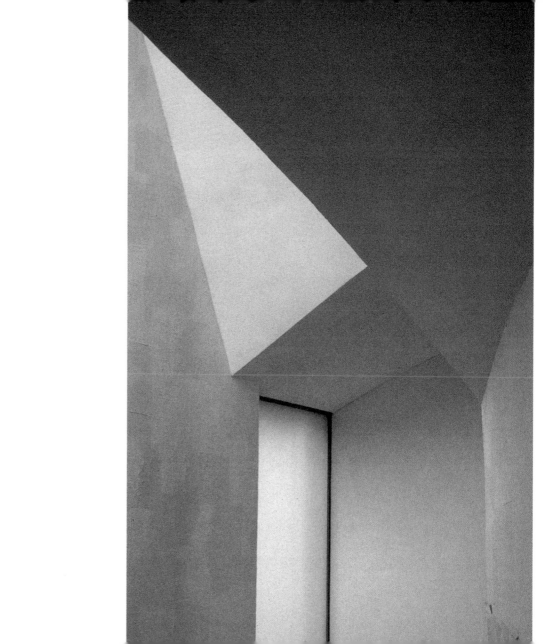

Sun-projected light from the colored lenses marks certain times of the day and year. Time, or duration, is a central theme of the interior. When clouds, typical in the Seattle sky, pass away from the face of the sun, a phenomenal "pulse" of reflected color occurs. This oscillating wave of reflected color, like a breath, invigorates the silent space.

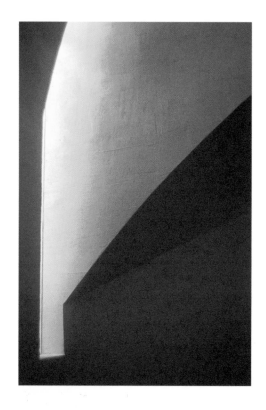 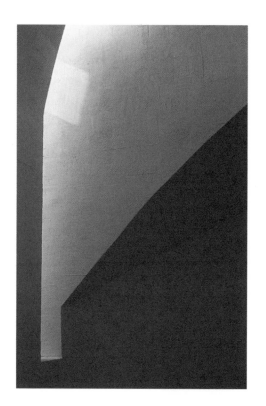 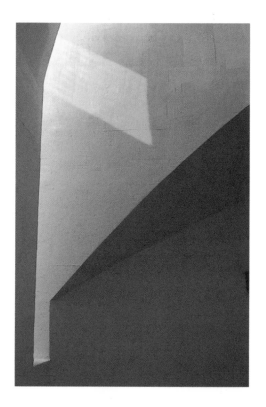

"What then is time? If no one asks me, I know; if I want to explain it to a questioner, I do not know.... We measure time. But how can we measure what does not exist? The past is no longer, the future is not yet. And what of the present? The present has not duration...when I measure time, I measure impressions, modifications of consciousness."

—Saint Augustine